BRAND BRILLIANCE

Building a Lasting Identity in the Marketplace

NANCY BARLOW

Copyright © 2024 by Nancy Barlow

All rights reserved. No part of this book may be reproduced, stored in a retrieval system, or transmitted, in any form or by any means, electronic, mechanical, photocopying, recording, or otherwise, without the prior written permission of the author, except in the case of brief quotations embodied in critical reviews and certain other noncommercial uses permitted by copyright law.

TABLE OF CONTENT

INTRODUCTION 5

CHAPTER 1: UNDERSTANDING BRAND IDENTITY 7

   - Defining Brand Identity 8

   - Importance of Consistency 11

   - Elements of Brand Identity: Logo, Colors, Typography 14

CHAPTER 2: CRAFTING YOUR BRAND STORY 19

   - Uncovering Your Brand's Purpose 20

   - Creating a Compelling Narrative 24

   - Communicating Values Effectively 28

CHAPTER 3: DESIGNING VISUAL BRAND ASSETS 33

   - Principles of Effective Design 34

   - Logo Design Strategies 38

   - Developing Brand Guidelines 42

CHAPTER 4: BUILDING BRAND EQUITY 49

- Establishing Brand Trust 50

- Leveraging Customer Experience 55

- Managing Brand Reputation 60

CHAPTER 5: ADAPTING TO MARKET DYNAMICS 67

- Navigating Competitive Landscapes 68

- Brand Evolution and Innovation 74

- Sustaining Brand Relevance Over Time 80

CONCLUSION 86

INTRODUCTION

"Brand Brilliance: Building a Lasting Identity in the Marketplace" delves into the art and science of crafting an enduring brand identity that resonates with audiences and stands the test of time. In an era where markets are saturated with options and competition is fierce, the ability to create a distinct and memorable brand is paramount for success.

This book is a comprehensive guide for entrepreneurs, marketers, and business leaders looking to navigate the complexities of brand development and positioning.

Throughout these pages, you'll uncover strategies and insights that go beyond the surface level, offering a deep dive into the core elements that shape a brand's identity. From defining your brand's purpose and values to crafting a compelling brand story and visual identity, each chapter is a roadmap towards achieving brand brilliance.

Drawing from real-world examples and case studies, this book provides actionable advice and practical tips that you can implement immediately. Whether you're launching a new brand or revitalizing an existing one, "Brand Brilliance" equips you with the knowledge and tools to build a strong, authentic, and enduring brand presence in today's dynamic marketplace. It's not just about standing out; it's about creating a lasting impact that resonates with your audience on a deeper level.

CHAPTER 1: UNDERSTANDING BRAND IDENTITY

In the intricate tapestry of the business world, one thread holds paramount importance: brand identity. Understanding Brand Identity is not just about recognizing logos and colors; it's about unraveling the core essence that distinguishes a brand in the marketplace. This chapter embarks on a journey into the heart of what makes a brand truly resonate with its audience. We'll delve deep into the foundational elements that shape perceptions, evoke emotions, and build lasting connections. From defining the very concept of brand identity to exploring the nuances of consistency and visual representation, this chapter lays the groundwork for crafting a brand that stands out amidst the noise. Join us as we navigate the intricate dance between strategy and creativity, unlocking the secrets to building a brand identity that not only captivates but endures in the ever-evolving landscape of business.

- Defining Brand Identity

Defining brand identity is like sculpting the essence of a brand, shaping its personality, values, and visual elements into a cohesive and recognizable entity. It's more than just a logo or a catchy tagline; it's the sum total of how a brand presents itself to the world and how it's perceived by its audience. Let's comprehensively discuss the components and importance of defining brand identity:

Components of Brand Identity

1. **Brand Purpose and Values:** At the core of every brand is its purpose - the reason it exists beyond making profits. Defining this purpose helps establish a brand's mission and values, guiding its actions and messaging.

2. **Brand Personality:** Brands often personify traits to connect with their target audience. Is your brand playful and energetic, or serious and professional? Defining this personality shapes how your brand communicates and engages.

3. **Brand Promise:** This is the commitment a brand makes to its customers. It encompasses what customers can expect from the brand, be it quality, innovation, reliability, or exceptional service.

4. **Target Audience:** Understanding who your brand serves is crucial. Define your ideal customer demographics, psychographics, and behaviors to tailor your messaging and offerings effectively.

5. **Brand Positioning:** How does your brand differentiate itself from competitors? Define your unique value proposition and positioning statement to clarify your brand's place in the market.

Importance of Defining Brand Identity

1. **Consistency:** A defined brand identity ensures consistency across all touchpoints, from marketing

materials to customer interactions, fostering trust and recognition.

2. **Memorability:** A well-defined brand identity creates a memorable impression, making it easier for customers to recall and choose your brand over others.

3. **Authenticity:** Clarity in brand identity helps convey authenticity, building emotional connections with customers who align with your brand's values and personality.

4. **Competitive Advantage:** A strong brand identity sets you apart from competitors, attracting and retaining customers who resonate with your brand's story and offerings.

5. **Longevity:** Brands with a clear and consistent identity are more likely to withstand market fluctuations and evolve sustainably over time.

In conclusion, defining brand identity is a strategic exercise that goes beyond superficial aesthetics. It's about crafting a compelling narrative, aligning with core values, and consistently delivering on promises to create a lasting impact on customers and the market.

- Importance of Consistency

Consistency is the cornerstone of a strong brand identity, playing a crucial role in shaping perceptions, building trust, and fostering brand loyalty. Let's comprehensively discuss the importance of consistency in brand identity:

1. **Establishes Trust and Reliability**

Consistency creates a sense of reliability and trustworthiness. When customers encounter consistent branding across various touchpoints such as website, social media, packaging, and customer service, they develop a sense of familiarity and confidence in the brand.

2. **Enhances Recognition and Recall**

Consistent branding elements, such as logo, colors, typography, and messaging, contribute to brand recognition. Customers can easily identify and remember a brand when they encounter consistent visuals and messaging, leading to increased recall and top-of-mind awareness.

3. Builds Brand Equity

Consistency contributes to building brand equity, which encompasses the intangible value and perception associated with a brand. Brands with strong consistency in their identity tend to command higher brand equity, leading to competitive advantages such as premium pricing and customer loyalty.

4. Supports Brand Differentiation

Consistency in brand identity helps differentiate a brand from competitors. When a brand maintains a consistent tone, style, and visual identity, it creates a unique and memorable experience for customers, setting itself apart in a crowded marketplace.

5. Improves Customer Experience

Consistency enhances the overall customer experience. When customers encounter consistent branding across all touchpoints, they experience a cohesive and seamless journey, leading to positive associations with the brand and increased satisfaction.

6. Facilitates Brand Communication

Consistency in brand identity simplifies brand communication. Clear and consistent branding elements make it easier for brands to convey their values, messaging, and offerings effectively to their target audience, resulting in better engagement and understanding.

7. Strengthens Brand Reputation

Consistency contributes to a positive brand reputation. Brands that consistently deliver on their promises and maintain a cohesive identity are perceived as more reliable, credible, and reputable by customers and stakeholders.

8. Supports Long-Term Growth

Consistency lays the foundation for long-term brand growth. Brands that prioritize consistency in their identity are better equipped to adapt to market changes, expand into new markets, and evolve their offerings while maintaining customer trust and loyalty.

In conclusion, consistency in brand identity is not just about visual uniformity; it's about building trust, enhancing recognition, differentiating from competitors, improving the customer experience, and ultimately, driving long-term success and growth for the brand.

- Elements of Brand Identity: Logo, Colors, Typography

1. Logo

The logo is a visual symbol that represents the essence of a brand. It is often the first point of contact between a brand and its audience, making it a critical element of brand identity.

- **Purpose:** The logo serves as a visual shorthand for the brand, encapsulating its values, personality, and offerings in a memorable and recognizable way.

- **Design:** A well-designed logo is simple, versatile, and scalable. It should be easily identifiable whether displayed on a billboard or a smartphone screen.

- **Consistency:** Consistency in logo usage across different platforms and applications reinforces brand recognition and strengthens brand identity.

2. Colors

Colors play a significant role in brand identity, evoking emotions, conveying messages, and creating visual appeal. A cohesive color palette enhances brand recognition and reinforces brand personality.

- **Brand Colors:** The selection of brand colors should align with the brand's personality, target audience preferences, and industry standards. Consistent use of these colors across all brand assets is crucial for brand consistency.

- **Psychology of Colors:** Different colors evoke different emotions and perceptions. Understanding color psychology helps brands choose colors that resonate with their audience and convey the desired brand image.

- **Color Usage Guidelines:** Establishing color usage guidelines ensures consistency in color application across various mediums. This includes specifying primary and secondary colors, as well as guidelines for background colors and color combinations.

3. **Typography**

Typography refers to the style, size, and arrangement of text elements used in brand communications. It plays a vital role in conveying brand voice, readability, and visual hierarchy.

- **Font Selection:** Choosing appropriate fonts that reflect the brand's personality and enhance readability is crucial. Brands often have primary and secondary fonts for different purposes, such as headlines, body text, and call-to-action elements.

- **Consistency in Typography:** Consistent use of typography across all brand materials maintains visual coherence and reinforces brand identity. Guidelines for font sizes, spacing, and text alignment contribute to a unified brand look.

- **Hierarchy and Emphasis:** Typography helps establish hierarchy and emphasis within content. Headlines, subheadings, and body text should be differentiated using font styles, sizes, and colors to guide the reader's attention and convey key messages effectively.

By carefully crafting and maintaining these elements of brand identity—logo, colors, and typography—brands can create a cohesive and compelling visual identity that resonates with their audience, fosters brand recognition, and strengthens brand loyalty.

CHAPTER 2: CRAFTING YOUR BRAND STORY

Crafting Your Brand Story is akin to weaving a narrative tapestry that connects your brand with its audience on a deeper level. In this chapter, we delve into the art and science of storytelling, exploring how to create a compelling and authentic brand narrative that resonates with your customers. Beyond products and services, your brand story is what sets you apart, evokes emotions, and builds lasting relationships.

We'll embark on a journey to uncover the essence of your brand—its purpose, values, and unique journey. By understanding the power of storytelling, you'll learn how to captivate your audience, communicate your brand's identity, and inspire action.

From defining your brand's purpose and crafting a narrative that reflects its core values to leveraging storytelling techniques that engage and connect, this chapter is your guide to crafting a brand story that not only captures attention but also leaves a lasting impact.

Join us as we explore the intricacies of storytelling in branding, unlocking the secrets to creating a brand narrative that resonates, inspires, and drives meaningful connections with your audience.

- Uncovering Your Brand's Purpose

Uncovering your brand's purpose is a transformative process that goes beyond profit-driven motives to define the fundamental reason for your brand's existence. It's about discovering the higher meaning and impact your brand aspires to make in the world. Let's comprehensively discuss the importance and steps involved in uncovering your brand's purpose:

Importance of Uncovering Brand Purpose

1. **Defines Brand Identity:** Your brand's purpose serves as the foundation of its identity, shaping its values, mission, and vision. It clarifies what your brand stands for and why it matters.

2. **Guides Decision-Making:** A clear brand purpose guides strategic decisions, from product development to marketing strategies. It ensures alignment with core values and long-term goals.

3. **Connects with Audiences:** Brands with a defined purpose resonate more deeply with customers who share similar values. It fosters emotional connections and loyalty.

4. **Inspires and Motivates:** Knowing your brand's purpose inspires employees, stakeholders, and customers. It gives meaning to their involvement with the brand beyond transactional interactions.

Steps to Uncover Brand Purpose

1. **Self-Reflection:** Start by reflecting on why your brand exists beyond making profits. What drives

you? What impact do you want to create in the world? Dig deep into your motivations and beliefs.

2. **Customer Understanding:** Understand your target audience's needs, aspirations, and values. How does your brand address their pain points or fulfill their desires? Align your purpose with customer insights.

3. **Competitive Analysis:** Evaluate your competitors' brand purposes. Identify gaps or opportunities where your brand can differentiate itself authentically.

4. **Core Values:** Define the core values that guide your brand's actions and decisions. These values should align with your purpose and resonate with both internal and external stakeholders.

5. **Crafting the Purpose Statement:** Use the insights gathered to craft a concise and inspiring purpose statement that encapsulates why your brand exists and the impact it aims to achieve.

6. **Integration Across Touchpoints:** Integrate your brand's purpose into every aspect of your business, from marketing communications to employee training. Consistency reinforces authenticity.

7. **Measurement and Adaptation:** Continuously measure the alignment of your brand's actions with its purpose. Adapt and refine strategies as needed to stay true to your purpose while meeting business objectives.

Examples of Strong Brand Purposes

1. **Nike:** "To bring inspiration and innovation to every athlete in the world. If you have a body, you are an athlete."

2. **Patagonia:** "Build the best product, cause no unnecessary harm, use business to inspire and implement solutions to the environmental crisis."

3. **Tesla:** "To accelerate the world's transition to sustainable energy."

In conclusion, uncovering your brand's purpose is a transformative journey that aligns your brand with meaningful impact and resonates with your audience on a deeper level. It's not just about what you sell but why you exist and the positive change you strive to create.

- Creating a Compelling Narrative

Creating a compelling narrative is an essential aspect of branding that goes beyond product features and benefits to engage customers emotionally and intellectually. A well-crafted brand narrative tells the story of your brand in a way that resonates with your audience, evokes emotions, and builds lasting connections. Let's comprehensively discuss the importance and key elements of creating a compelling narrative:

Importance of Creating a Compelling Narrative

1. **Emotional Connection:** A compelling narrative taps into emotions, making your brand more relatable and memorable to customers. It creates a bond that goes beyond transactional relationships.

2. **Differentiation:** In a competitive market, a unique brand narrative sets you apart from competitors by showcasing your brand's personality, values, and vision.

3. **Engagement:** Stories have the power to captivate and hold attention. A compelling narrative keeps your audience engaged, leading to increased brand recall and loyalty.

4. **Authenticity:** Authentic storytelling builds trust with customers. When your narrative aligns with your brand's actions and values, it enhances credibility and transparency.

5. **Influence and Persuasion:** Stories have a persuasive impact on decision-making. A well-crafted narrative can influence perceptions, attitudes, and purchasing behavior.

Key Elements of Creating a Compelling Narrative

1. **Character Development:** Every compelling narrative has characters that drive the story. Your brand can be the protagonist, but also consider how

customers, employees, and partners play roles in your narrative.

2. **Conflict and Resolution:** A narrative without conflict lacks intrigue. Identify challenges or problems your brand addresses and highlight how your solutions bring resolution.

3. **Purpose and Mission:** Communicate your brand's purpose and mission clearly in the narrative. Show how your brand is on a meaningful journey to create positive change or fulfill a greater purpose.

4. **Emotional Appeal:** Use emotions to connect with your audience. Whether it's humor, empathy, inspiration, or nostalgia, evoke feelings that resonate with your brand's values and story.

5. **Visual Storytelling:** Combine words with visuals to enhance your narrative. Use imagery, videos, and graphics that reinforce your brand's story and create a compelling visual experience.

6. **Consistency:** Maintain consistency in storytelling across all brand touchpoints. From marketing campaigns to customer interactions,

ensure that your narrative remains cohesive and aligned with your brand identity.

Examples of Compelling Brand Narratives

1. **Dove's Campaign for Real Beauty:** Dove's narrative challenges beauty stereotypes and promotes self-acceptance, resonating with diverse audiences globally.

2. **Apple's "Think Different" Campaign:** Apple's narrative celebrates innovation, creativity, and individuality, positioning the brand as a symbol of cutting-edge technology and design.

3. **Airbnb's "Belong Anywhere" Story:** Airbnb's narrative focuses on creating connections and cultural experiences, fostering a sense of belonging for travelers worldwide.

In conclusion, creating a compelling narrative is a powerful tool for brands to connect with their audience, differentiate themselves, and inspire action. By weaving together storytelling elements that resonate emotionally, authentically, and consistently, brands can create a lasting impact and forge meaningful relationships with customers.

- Communicating Values Effectively

Communicating values effectively is a cornerstone of successful branding, as it helps establish a strong connection with customers, differentiate your brand, and build trust and loyalty. Let's comprehensively discuss the importance and strategies for communicating values effectively:

Importance of Communicating Values

1. **Builds Trust and Credibility:** When you communicate your values authentically and consistently, you build trust with customers. They are more likely to support a brand that shares their values and beliefs.

2. **Differentiation:** Values-based communication helps differentiate your brand from competitors. It

showcases what sets your brand apart and why customers should choose you over alternatives.

3. **Attracts Like-Minded Customers:** Effective values communication attracts customers who share similar values. This creates a sense of belonging and fosters stronger relationships with your target audience.

4. **Guides Decision-Making:** Values serve as a compass for decision-making within your organization. Communicating these values helps align actions and behaviors with your brand's mission and vision.

5. **Creates Emotional Connections:** Values-based communication taps into emotions, creating meaningful connections with customers. Emotional connections lead to higher customer satisfaction and loyalty.

Strategies for Communicating Values Effectively

1. **Clarity and Consistency:** Clearly define your brand values and ensure consistency in how you

communicate them across all touchpoints. This includes marketing materials, social media, customer interactions, and internal communications.

2. **Storytelling:** Use storytelling to bring your values to life. Share real-life examples, customer stories, and experiences that demonstrate how your values guide your actions and decisions.

3. **Visual Representation:** Use visuals such as graphics, images, and videos to reinforce your brand values visually. Visual elements can evoke emotions and make values more memorable.

4. **Employee Advocacy:** Your employees are ambassadors of your brand values. Encourage and empower them to embody and communicate these values in their interactions with customers and stakeholders.

5. **Transparency:** Be transparent about your values, including how they influence your business practices, product development, and social impact. Transparency builds trust and credibility with customers.

6. **Community Engagement:** Engage with your community and stakeholders on topics related to your values. Participate in relevant conversations, support causes aligned with your values, and demonstrate your commitment to making a positive impact.

7. **Customer Feedback:** Listen to customer feedback regarding your values communication. Use insights to refine your messaging and ensure it resonates with your target audience.

Examples of Effective Values Communication

1. **Patagonia:** Patagonia effectively communicates its values of environmental sustainability and activism through campaigns, product messaging, and partnerships with environmental organizations.

2. **Ben & Jerry's:** Ben & Jerry's communicates its values of social justice, equality, and sustainability through product names, flavors, and advocacy campaigns on issues like climate change and social justice.

3. Tesla: Tesla communicates its values of innovation, sustainability, and clean energy through product features, marketing campaigns, and CEO Elon Musk's public statements on the importance of renewable energy.

In conclusion, communicating values effectively is essential for building trust, differentiation, and emotional connections with customers. By defining clear values, using storytelling and visual elements, engaging stakeholders, and demonstrating transparency, brands can effectively convey their values and create a meaningful impact in the marketplace.

CHAPTER 3: DESIGNING VISUAL BRAND ASSETS

Designing Visual Brand Assets is like painting the canvas of your brand's identity. In this chapter, we delve into the visual elements that play a pivotal role in shaping how your brand is perceived and remembered. From logos and color palettes to typography and imagery, every visual aspect contributes to crafting a cohesive and impactful brand presence.

This chapter explores the principles of effective design, the psychology of colors, and the art of creating visually compelling brand assets. Whether you're designing a logo that encapsulates your brand's essence or developing brand guidelines to ensure visual consistency, this chapter serves as your guide to creating visual brand assets that resonate with your audience and leave a lasting impression.

Join us as we navigate the world of visual storytelling, uncovering the strategies and techniques that elevate your brand's visual identity and strengthen its connection with customers. Through a blend of creativity, strategy, and attention to detail, you'll learn how to design visual brand assets that not only stand out but also communicate your brand's values, personality, and promise effectively.

- Principles of Effective Design

Principles of effective design are fundamental guidelines that govern the creation of visually appealing and functional designs across various mediums, including graphic design, web design, product design, and branding. These principles are essential for creating designs that are not only aesthetically pleasing but also communicate effectively and enhance user experience. Let's comprehensively discuss the key principles of effective design:

1. **Balance**

- **Symmetrical Balance:** Achieved when elements are mirrored or evenly distributed on both sides of a central axis, creating a sense of stability and order.

- **Asymmetrical Balance:** Involves arranging elements of different sizes and visual weights to achieve balance through contrast and composition.

2. **Hierarchy**

- Establishes a visual order of importance within a design by using size, color, contrast, and placement to guide the viewer's eye and prioritize information.

3. **Contrast**

- Creates visual interest and emphasis by juxtaposing elements with differing characteristics such as color, size, shape, or texture.

- Effective use of contrast enhances readability, draws attention to key elements, and adds depth to the design.

4. **Emphasis**

- Highlights focal points or key elements in a design to attract attention and convey hierarchy.

- Techniques for creating emphasis include size, color, typography, whitespace, and placement.

5. **Unity**

- Ensures that all elements in a design work harmoniously together to create a cohesive and unified visual experience.

- Consistent use of design elements, such as colors, fonts, and imagery, contributes to unity.

6. **Proportion and Scale**

- Proportion refers to the relative size and scale of elements within a design, ensuring that they are visually pleasing and balanced.

- Scale involves varying the size of elements to create hierarchy, contrast, and visual interest.

7. Typography

- Involves the selection, arrangement, and use of typefaces to enhance readability, convey tone and personality, and establish hierarchy.

- Considerations include font choice, size, spacing, alignment, and hierarchy of text elements.

8. Color Theory

- Understanding color psychology, color harmony, and color meanings to evoke emotions, convey messages, and create visual impact.

- Principles such as complementary colors, analogous colors, and color contrast are used to achieve effective color schemes.

9. Whitespace

- Also known as negative space, whitespace refers to the areas of a design that are intentionally left blank.

- Proper use of whitespace improves readability, emphasizes key elements, and enhances visual clarity and breathing room.

10. **Consistency**

- Maintaining consistency in design elements, styles, and branding across all materials and platforms to reinforce brand identity, recognition, and trust.

By applying these principles of effective design thoughtfully and strategically, designers can create visually compelling and impactful designs that engage users, communicate messages clearly, and achieve desired objectives across various design disciplines.

- Logo Design Strategies

Logo design strategies encompass a range of considerations and techniques aimed at creating a visually impactful and memorable symbol that represents a brand's identity. A well-designed logo is essential for brand recognition, differentiation, and communicating the essence of a brand to its audience. Let's comprehensively discuss key logo design strategies:

1. **Understand Brand Identity**

   - Begin by understanding the brand's identity, values, mission, and target audience. The logo should reflect these elements to resonate with customers effectively.

2. **Simplicity**

   - Keep the design simple and uncluttered. A minimalist approach ensures clarity and makes the logo easy to recognize and remember.

3. **Versatility**

   - Design a logo that works well across various mediums and sizes, from digital platforms to print materials. It should be scalable without losing clarity or impact.

4. Timelessness

- Aim for a design that stands the test of time. Avoid trendy elements that may quickly become outdated, opting for a timeless and enduring look.

5. Uniqueness

- Ensure that the logo is distinct and differentiates the brand from competitors. A unique design helps create a memorable impression and fosters brand recall.

6. Relevance

- Make sure the logo is relevant to the industry, market, and target audience. It should align with the brand's products, services, and brand personality.

7. Scalability

- Consider how the logo will appear across different platforms, devices, and sizes. Test its visibility and legibility at various scales to ensure optimal performance.

8. Color and Typography

- Choose colors and typography that complement the brand's identity and convey the desired message. Consider the psychological impact of colors and the readability of typography.

9. Adaptability

- Design the logo to be adaptable for different applications, such as color variations, monochrome versions, and reversed options for light and dark backgrounds.

10. Meaning and Storytelling

- Incorporate elements or symbols that have meaning and relevance to the brand's story, history, values, or industry. A well-designed logo tells a story and evokes emotions.

11. Feedback and Iteration

- Seek feedback from stakeholders, designers, and target audience members. Iterate on the design based on feedback to refine and improve the logo.

12. Legal Considerations

- Ensure that the logo design is original and does not infringe on trademarks or copyrights. Consult legal experts if needed to protect intellectual property rights.

By following these logo design strategies, designers can create logos that not only visually represent the brand but also effectively communicate its identity, values, and message to the audience, contributing to brand recognition, loyalty, and success.

- Developing Brand Guidelines

Developing brand guidelines is a crucial step in ensuring consistency, coherence, and effective communication of a brand's identity across various touchpoints. Brand guidelines serve as a comprehensive document that outlines the visual, verbal, and experiential aspects of a brand, providing clear instructions and standards for internal and external stakeholders. Let's comprehensively discuss the key components and steps involved in developing brand guidelines:

Key Components of Brand Guidelines

1. **Brand Identity**

- **Logo:** Guidelines for logo usage, variations, spacing, sizing, color options, and clear space.

- **Color Palette:** Defined primary and secondary colors, color codes (RGB, CMYK, HEX), and guidelines for color usage.

- **Typography:** Specified fonts, font sizes, font weights, and guidelines for headings, body text, and other text elements.

- **Imagery:** Guidelines for the use of photography, illustrations, icons, and graphics that align with the brand's style and tone.

2. **Brand Voice and Tone**

- **Voice:** Defined personality traits (e.g., friendly, professional, authoritative) and guidelines for writing style, language, and tone of voice.

- **Messaging:** Key messaging pillars, brand stories, taglines, and guidelines for crafting effective communication across channels.

3. **Design Elements**

  - **Layouts:** Guidelines for layout grids, margins, padding, and visual hierarchy to maintain consistency in design across materials.

  - **Icons and Graphics:** Standardized icons, graphics, and visual elements that reflect the brand's style and enhance communication.

  - **Templates:** Design templates for presentations, documents, social media posts, and other branded materials.

4. **Brand Usage**

  - **Brand Applications:** Guidelines for applying the brand identity across various applications, such as digital platforms, print materials, merchandise, and packaging.

- **Logo Misuse:** Examples of incorrect logo usage and instructions on what to avoid to maintain brand integrity.

- **Brand Partnerships:** Guidelines for co-branding, sponsorships, and collaborations to ensure consistent brand representation.

5. **Brand Experience**

- **Customer Experience:** Standards for delivering a consistent brand experience at touchpoints like customer service, product packaging, and user interfaces.

- **Brand Values:** Integration of brand values, mission, and vision into every aspect of the brand experience to reinforce authenticity and trust.

Steps to Develop Brand Guidelines

1. **Research and Analysis**

- Conduct market research, competitor analysis, and audience research to understand brand positioning, target audience preferences, and industry standards.

2. **Define Brand Identity**

   - Define the brand's visual identity, voice, tone, values, and personality traits that align with the brand's mission and resonate with the target audience.

3. **Create Visual Assets**

   - Design and create visual assets such as logos, color palettes, typography styles, imagery, and brand collateral that reflect the brand identity.

4. **Document Guidelines**

   - Compile all brand elements, guidelines, and standards into a comprehensive brand guidelines document that is accessible and easy to reference for stakeholders.

5. **Educate and Implement**

   - Educate internal teams, partners, and stakeholders on the brand guidelines and ensure their understanding and adherence to maintain consistency in brand representation.

6. **Regular Review and Update**

- Regularly review and update the brand guidelines document to incorporate changes, new assets, and evolving brand strategies while ensuring consistency and relevance.

Benefits of Brand Guidelines

1. **Consistency:** Ensures consistent brand representation across all channels, materials, and touchpoints, reinforcing brand recognition and trust.

2. **Clarity:** Provides clear instructions and standards for internal teams, agencies, and partners, reducing confusion and ensuring brand integrity.

3. **Efficiency:** Streamlines the design and communication process by providing templates, assets, and guidelines, saving time and resources.

4. **Brand Protection:** Safeguards the brand's identity and reputation by preventing misuse, unauthorized alterations, and inconsistent branding.

5. **Brand Cohesion:** Fosters a cohesive brand experience that resonates with customers, builds loyalty, and strengthens brand equity.

By developing comprehensive brand guidelines that encompass all aspects of the brand identity and experience, organizations can effectively communicate their brand's story, values, and personality while maintaining consistency and coherence across diverse channels and audiences.

CHAPTER 4: BUILDING BRAND EQUITY

Building Brand Equity is akin to cultivating a valuable asset that represents the sum of a brand's reputation, recognition, and perceived value. In this chapter, we delve into the strategies and practices that contribute to strengthening and enhancing brand equity—the intangible but highly influential asset that drives customer loyalty, competitive advantage, and long-term success.

From establishing brand identity and delivering exceptional customer experiences to leveraging effective marketing strategies and maintaining brand consistency, this chapter serves as a guide to building and nurturing brand equity. We'll explore the significance of brand equity, key drivers, measurement metrics, and actionable steps for brands to enhance their equity and create lasting connections with customers.

Join us on this journey as we uncover the principles and tactics that empower brands to elevate their value, resonate with their target audience, and establish a strong and enduring presence in the marketplace. Through strategic brand building initiatives, organizations can cultivate brand equity that not only drives business growth but also fosters trust, loyalty, and advocacy among consumers.

- Establishing Brand Trust

Establishing brand trust is essential for building strong and lasting relationships with customers, fostering loyalty, and driving business success. Trust is the foundation upon which positive brand perceptions, credibility, and customer satisfaction are built. Let's comprehensively discuss the strategies and factors involved in establishing brand trust:

1. **Consistent Brand Identity**

- **Brand Promise:** Clearly define and communicate what your brand stands for, its values, mission, and commitments to customers.

- **Brand Voice:** Maintain a consistent tone, style, and messaging across all communications to reinforce brand personality and authenticity.

2. **Quality and Reliability**

- **Product/Service Excellence:** Deliver high-quality products or services that meet or exceed customer expectations consistently.

- **Consistent Performance:** Ensure reliability in delivering promises, meeting deadlines, and providing consistent customer experiences.

3. **Transparency and Honesty**

- **Open Communication:** Be transparent about business practices, pricing, policies, and product/service information to build credibility and trust.

- **Honest Marketing:** Avoid misleading or deceptive marketing tactics; provide accurate information and set realistic expectations.

4. Customer-Centric Approach

- **Empathy:** Understand and empathize with customer needs, concerns, and feedback to demonstrate genuine care and responsiveness.

- **Personalization:** Tailor experiences, offers, and communications to individual preferences and interests to show appreciation and respect.

5. Social Responsibility

- **Ethical Practices:** Demonstrate ethical behavior, social responsibility, and environmental sustainability practices that align with customer values.

- **Community Engagement:** Engage in philanthropic efforts, support causes, and contribute positively to communities to build goodwill and trust.

6. Consistent Brand Experience

- **Omni-channel Experience:** Ensure a seamless and consistent experience across all touchpoints, including online platforms, physical stores, customer service, and marketing channels.

- **Brand Consistency:** Maintain consistency in branding elements, visual identity, messaging, and customer interactions to reinforce brand recall and trust.

7. Customer Feedback and Improvement

- **Feedback Loop:** Encourage and listen to customer feedback, reviews, and suggestions to understand areas for improvement and demonstrate responsiveness.

- **Continuous Improvement:** Act on feedback, address issues promptly, and strive for continuous improvement in products, services, and customer experiences.

8. Influencer and Social Proof

- **Testimonials and Reviews:** Showcase positive customer testimonials, reviews, and endorsements to build social proof and credibility.

- **Influencer Partnerships**: Collaborate with credible influencers or brand advocates to amplify trust and reach among their audiences.

9. Crisis Management

- **Transparency in Crisis:** In times of crisis or challenges, communicate openly, take responsibility, and show accountability to maintain trust and credibility.

- **Recovery Efforts:** Implement effective recovery strategies, compensate for mistakes, and learn from incidents to rebuild trust.

10. Long-term Relationship Building

- **Customer Engagement:** Foster ongoing engagement, communication, and relationship-building initiatives to nurture long-term connections and loyalty.

- **Consistent Value Delivery:** Continuously provide value, benefits, and positive experiences to reinforce trust and loyalty over time.

By implementing these strategies and prioritizing trust-building initiatives, brands can cultivate strong, resilient relationships with customers, enhance brand reputation, and create a competitive advantage in the market.

- Leveraging Customer Experience

Leveraging customer experience (CX) is a strategic approach that focuses on creating positive, memorable interactions and relationships with customers throughout their journey with a brand. CX encompasses every touchpoint and interaction a customer has with a brand, from initial awareness to post-purchase support. Let's comprehensively discuss the importance, strategies, and benefits of leveraging customer experience:

Importance of Leveraging Customer Experience

1. **Customer Satisfaction:** Positive experiences lead to higher levels of customer satisfaction, loyalty, and advocacy, fostering repeat business and referrals.

2. **Competitive Advantage:** Exceptional CX sets brands apart from competitors, as customers are more likely to choose brands that prioritize their needs and deliver superior experiences.

3. **Brand Loyalty:** Building strong emotional connections and trust through CX initiatives increases customer loyalty and reduces churn rates.

4. **Revenue Growth:** Satisfied and loyal customers tend to spend more, contribute to higher lifetime value, and act as brand ambassadors, driving revenue growth.

Strategies for Leveraging Customer Experience

1. Understand Customer Journey

- Map the customer journey to identify touchpoints, pain points, and opportunities to enhance the overall experience.

2. Personalization

- Tailor experiences, content, and offerings based on customer preferences, behaviors, and past interactions to create personalized experiences.

3. Consistent Omnichannel Experience

- Ensure seamless and consistent experiences across all channels, including online platforms, physical stores, mobile apps, and customer support.

4. Empathy and Engagement

- Show empathy, actively listen to customer feedback, and engage in meaningful interactions to address needs and build trust.

5. **Proactive Support**

   - Anticipate customer needs and provide proactive support, recommendations, and solutions to enhance satisfaction and loyalty.

6. **Employee Training and Empowerment**

   - Train and empower frontline employees to deliver exceptional service, resolve issues efficiently, and create positive interactions with customers.

7. **Continuous Improvement**

   - Gather and analyze customer feedback, metrics, and insights to identify areas for improvement and implement changes to enhance CX.

8. **Innovative Technology**

   - Leverage technology such as AI, chatbots, CRM systems, and data analytics to streamline processes, personalize experiences, and deliver real-time support.

9. **Reward and Recognition**

- Recognize and reward loyal customers, advocate programs, and provide incentives to encourage repeat business and referrals.

10. **Community Building**

- Build a community of loyal customers, brand advocates, and influencers to foster engagement, loyalty, and word-of-mouth marketing.

Benefits of Leveraging Customer Experience

1. **Higher Customer Satisfaction:** Positive experiences lead to increased satisfaction, loyalty, and advocacy.

2. **Improved Brand Reputation:** Consistently delivering excellent CX enhances brand reputation and credibility.

3. **Increased Revenue:** Satisfied and loyal customers contribute to higher revenue, repeat business, and customer lifetime value.

4. **Competitive Advantage:** Superior CX sets brands apart from competitors and attracts new customers through positive word-of-mouth.

5. **Enhanced Employee Satisfaction:** Employees are more engaged and motivated when they deliver exceptional CX, leading to higher productivity and retention.

By prioritizing and investing in customer experience initiatives, brands can create meaningful, long-lasting relationships with customers, drive business growth, and maintain a competitive edge in the market.

- Managing Brand Reputation

Managing brand reputation is crucial for building trust, credibility, and positive perceptions among customers, stakeholders, and the public. Brand reputation encompasses how a brand is perceived based on its actions, communications, customer experiences, and overall conduct. Let's comprehensively discuss the importance, strategies, and benefits of managing brand reputation effectively:

Importance of Managing Brand Reputation

1. **Trust and Credibility:** A positive reputation builds trust with customers, stakeholders, investors, and partners, enhancing brand credibility and loyalty.

2. **Customer Perception:** Reputation influences how customers perceive and interact with a brand, affecting purchase decisions, brand advocacy, and long-term relationships.

3. **Competitive Advantage:** A strong reputation sets brands apart from competitors, attracts new customers, and retains existing ones through positive word-of-mouth and referrals.

4. **Crisis Resilience:** Proactively managing reputation prepares brands to respond effectively to crises, negative publicity, and challenges, minimizing damage and restoring trust.

5. **Brand Equity**: A positive reputation contributes to brand equity, which encompasses the intangible value and assets associated with a brand, including customer loyalty and premium pricing.

Strategies for Managing Brand Reputation

1. **Build a Strong Brand Identity**

   - Define brand values, mission, vision, and personality that align with customer expectations and market trends.

   - Consistently communicate and demonstrate brand values through actions, messages, and experiences.

2. **Monitor Online Reputation**

   - Use tools and platforms to monitor online mentions, reviews, social media conversations, and news articles related to the brand.

   - Address negative feedback promptly, engage with customers, and seek opportunities to resolve issues and improve.

3. **Provide Excellent Customer Experiences**

- Prioritize customer satisfaction and deliver exceptional experiences at every touchpoint.

- Listen to customer feedback, address concerns, and exceed expectations to build positive relationships.

4. **Transparency and Authenticity**

- Be transparent in communication, operations, and decision-making processes.

- Acknowledge mistakes, take responsibility, and demonstrate authenticity in actions and messaging.

5. **Manage Crisis Effectively**

- Develop a crisis management plan with clear protocols, designated spokespeople, and response strategies.

- Communicate openly, honestly, and promptly during crises, focusing on resolution and rebuilding trust.

6. **Invest in Public Relations**

   - Develop positive relationships with media, influencers, industry experts, and community leaders.

   - Proactively engage in PR efforts, events, sponsorships, and partnerships to enhance brand visibility and reputation.

7. **Employee Advocacy**

   - Empower and train employees to be brand advocates, aligning with brand values and promoting positive narratives.

   - Foster a positive workplace culture, communication channels, and employee engagement initiatives.

8. **Monitor and Adapt**

   - Continuously monitor brand sentiment, market trends, and competitive landscape to adapt strategies and messaging accordingly.

- Stay agile and responsive to changes, feedback, and emerging issues to maintain a positive brand image.

Benefits of Managing Brand Reputation

1. **Enhanced Trust and Loyalty:** Positive reputation builds trust, loyalty, and long-term relationships with customers and stakeholders.

2. **Increased Customer Acquisition:** A strong reputation attracts new customers, improves conversion rates, and drives business growth.

3. **Crisis Resilience:** Effective reputation management prepares brands to navigate crises, challenges, and negative publicity with resilience and credibility.

4. **Brand Differentiation:** Positive reputation sets brands apart from competitors, creating a unique selling proposition and competitive advantage.

5. **Brand Equity:** Reputation contributes to brand equity, influencing customer perceptions,

willingness to pay premium prices, and overall brand value.

By implementing proactive reputation management strategies, brands can strengthen their position in the market, build enduring relationships with stakeholders, and sustain long-term success.

CHAPTER 5: ADAPTING TO MARKET DYNAMICS

Adapting to market dynamics is a strategic imperative for businesses aiming to thrive in today's rapidly evolving and competitive landscape. Market dynamics encompass the ever-changing forces, trends, and conditions that impact industries, consumer behavior, technology, and global markets. In this chapter, we delve into the strategies, challenges, and opportunities involved in effectively adapting to market dynamics.

From understanding market trends and consumer preferences to embracing innovation, agility, and resilience, this chapter serves as a guide for businesses seeking to navigate and capitalize on market shifts. We'll explore the importance of market intelligence, proactive decision-making, strategic planning, and flexible business models in responding to changing market conditions.

Join us as we explore the dynamic nature of markets, uncover actionable insights, and discuss best practices for staying competitive, relevant, and successful amidst market fluctuations. Through adaptive strategies and a forward-thinking mindset, businesses can not only survive but also thrive in dynamic and uncertain environments, driving growth, and sustainable success.

- Navigating Competitive Landscapes

Navigating competitive landscapes is essential for businesses to understand their market position, identify opportunities, and develop strategies to thrive in competitive environments. Competitive landscapes encompass the array of competitors, market dynamics, industry trends, and customer preferences that influence business performance. Let's comprehensively discuss the importance, strategies, and benefits of navigating competitive landscapes effectively:

Importance of Navigating Competitive Landscapes

1. **Market Understanding:** Understanding competitors, their strengths, weaknesses, and market strategies helps businesses make informed decisions and stay competitive.

2. **Opportunity Identification:** Analyzing competitive landscapes reveals market gaps, emerging trends, and areas for innovation and differentiation.

3. **Strategic Planning:** Insights from competitive analysis inform strategic planning, market positioning, pricing strategies, product development, and marketing efforts.

4. **Risk Mitigation:** Awareness of competitive threats and market dynamics enables businesses to anticipate challenges, mitigate risks, and capitalize on opportunities.

5. **Customer-Centric Approach:** Analyzing competitors' offerings and customer feedback helps businesses align products, services, and experiences with customer needs and preferences.

Strategies for Navigating Competitive Landscapes

1. **Competitor Analysis**

   - Identify direct and indirect competitors, assess their market share, strengths, weaknesses, pricing strategies, product offerings, and market positioning.

   - Conduct SWOT analysis (Strengths, Weaknesses, Opportunities, Threats) to identify key insights and competitive advantages.

2. **Market Research**

   - Gather market intelligence, industry trends, consumer behavior, and customer feedback to understand market dynamics, emerging opportunities, and threats.

- Use tools, surveys, interviews, and data analysis to gain actionable insights into customer preferences, pain points, and buying behaviors.

3. **Differentiation and Innovation**

   - Identify unique selling propositions (USPs) and areas for differentiation based on customer needs, market gaps, and competitors' offerings.

   - Invest in innovation, product development, and continuous improvement to stay ahead of competitors and meet evolving customer expectations.

4. **Strategic Partnerships and Alliances**

   - Collaborate with strategic partners, suppliers, distributors, and industry stakeholders to access new markets, resources, capabilities, and growth opportunities.

   - Leverage partnerships for co-marketing initiatives, joint ventures, and expanding market reach.

5. **Agility and Flexibility**

  - Foster agility and adaptability in response to market changes, customer feedback, and competitive dynamics.

  - Develop contingency plans, scenario analysis, and risk management strategies to navigate uncertainties and disruptions effectively.

6. **Brand Positioning and Marketing**

  - Define a clear brand identity, value proposition, and messaging that resonate with target customers and differentiate from competitors.

  - Implement targeted marketing strategies, digital marketing campaigns, and customer engagement initiatives to build brand awareness, loyalty, and competitive advantage.

7. **Customer Experience Excellence**

  - Prioritize customer experience (CX) by delivering exceptional service, personalized experiences, and seamless interactions across all touchpoints.

- Use customer feedback, analytics, and metrics to continuously improve CX, address pain points, and enhance customer satisfaction.

Benefits of Navigating Competitive Landscapes

1. **Strategic Advantage:** Strategic insights from competitive analysis inform decision-making, market positioning, and competitive advantage.

2. **Innovation and Differentiation:** Understanding market gaps and customer needs fosters innovation, differentiation, and product development.

3. **Market Opportunities:** Identify emerging trends, untapped markets, and growth opportunities to capitalize on market dynamics and expand market share.

4. **Risk Management:** Anticipate competitive threats, market disruptions, and industry changes to mitigate risks and make proactive adjustments.

5. **Customer-Centric Approach:** Align strategies, products, and experiences with customer

preferences, driving customer satisfaction, loyalty, and retention.

By implementing proactive strategies and staying informed about competitive landscapes, businesses can effectively navigate challenges, capitalize on opportunities, and achieve sustainable growth and success in dynamic and competitive markets.

- Brand Evolution and Innovation

Brand evolution and innovation are fundamental to staying relevant, competitive, and resilient in dynamic market environments. Brands that evolve and innovate effectively can adapt to changing consumer preferences, technological advancements, and market trends, ensuring long-term success and growth. Let's comprehensively discuss the importance, strategies, and benefits of brand evolution and innovation:

Importance of Brand Evolution and Innovation

1. **Relevance:** Evolving brands stay relevant to changing customer needs, preferences, and expectations, maintaining a strong connection with target audiences.

2. **Competitive Advantage:** Innovative brands differentiate themselves from competitors, attract new customers, and retain existing ones through unique offerings and experiences.

3. **Adaptability:** Brands that evolve and innovate can adapt to market shifts, disruptions, and emerging trends, staying agile and competitive.

4. **Brand Resilience:** Continuous innovation builds brand resilience, enabling brands to withstand challenges, disruptions, and industry changes.

5. **Customer Engagement:** Innovative brands foster customer engagement, loyalty, and advocacy by offering novel experiences, products, and solutions.

Strategies for Brand Evolution and Innovation

1. **Market Research and Insights**

   - Conduct market research, trend analysis, and consumer surveys to gather insights into market dynamics, customer preferences, and industry trends.

   - Use data analytics, customer feedback, and competitive analysis to identify opportunities for innovation and brand evolution.

2. **Customer-Centric Approach**

   - Put customers at the center of brand evolution and innovation efforts, understanding their needs, pain points, aspirations, and feedback.

   - Develop empathy maps, personas, and customer journey maps to gain deep insights into customer experiences and expectations.

3. **Product and Service Innovation**

- Invest in product development, design thinking, and prototyping to create innovative products, services, features, and solutions.

- Embrace technology advancements, digital transformation, and IoT (Internet of Things) to enhance offerings and customer experiences.

4. **Brand Identity and Positioning**

- Evolve brand identity, values, messaging, and positioning to reflect evolving market trends, customer values, and competitive landscape.

- Rebranding, brand refresh, or brand extensions can reinvigorate brand perception and attract new audiences.

5. **Collaboration and Partnerships**

- Collaborate with industry partners, startups, innovators, and experts to access new ideas, technologies, resources, and market opportunities.

- Joint ventures, co-creation projects, and innovation hubs foster creativity, knowledge sharing, and cross-functional collaboration.

6. **Agility and Experimentation**

- Foster a culture of agility, experimentation, and risk-taking within the organization to encourage innovation and continuous improvement.

- Implement agile methodologies, rapid prototyping, and iterative development to test and iterate new ideas and concepts quickly.

7. **Marketing and Communication**

- Develop innovative marketing campaigns, storytelling, and content strategies that resonate with target audiences and showcase brand evolution.

- Leverage digital marketing, social media, influencer partnerships, and experiential marketing to amplify brand innovation and reach.

Benefits of Brand Evolution and Innovation

1. **Competitive Differentiation:** Innovative brands differentiate themselves from competitors, creating a unique selling proposition and competitive advantage.

2. **Customer Loyalty and Advocacy:** Brand evolution and innovation build customer loyalty, satisfaction, and advocacy through novel experiences, products, and solutions.

3. **Market Expansion:** New offerings and innovations open doors to new markets, customer segments, revenue streams, and business opportunities.

4. **Brand Resilience:** Adaptive brands are resilient to market changes, disruptions, and challenges, ensuring sustainability and long-term success.

5. **Organizational Growth: A** culture of innovation and brand evolution fosters employee engagement, creativity, and organizational growth.

By embracing brand evolution and innovation as strategic imperatives, brands can stay ahead of the curve, delight customers, drive growth, and achieve sustainable success in rapidly evolving markets.

- Sustaining Brand Relevance Over Time

Brand evolution and innovation are fundamental to staying relevant, competitive, and resilient in dynamic market environments. Brands that evolve and innovate effectively can adapt to changing consumer preferences, technological advancements, and market trends, ensuring long-term success and growth. Let's comprehensively discuss the importance, strategies, and benefits of brand evolution and innovation:

Importance of Brand Evolution and Innovation

1. **Relevance:** Evolving brands stay relevant to changing customer needs, preferences, and expectations, maintaining a strong connection with target audiences.

2. **Competitive Advantage**: Innovative brands differentiate themselves from competitors, attract new customers, and retain existing ones through unique offerings and experiences.

3. **Adaptability:** Brands that evolve and innovate can adapt to market shifts, disruptions, and emerging trends, staying agile and competitive.

4. **Brand Resilience:** Continuous innovation builds brand resilience, enabling brands to withstand challenges, disruptions, and industry changes.

5. **Customer Engagement:** Innovative brands foster customer engagement, loyalty, and advocacy by offering novel experiences, products, and solutions.

Strategies for Brand Evolution and Innovation

1. **Market Research and Insights**

   - Conduct market research, trend analysis, and consumer surveys to gather insights into market dynamics, customer preferences, and industry trends.

- Use data analytics, customer feedback, and competitive analysis to identify opportunities for innovation and brand evolution.

2. Customer-Centric Approach

- Put customers at the center of brand evolution and innovation efforts, understanding their needs, pain points, aspirations, and feedback.

- Develop empathy maps, personas, and customer journey maps to gain deep insights into customer experiences and expectations.

3. Product and Service Innovation

- Invest in product development, design thinking, and prototyping to create innovative products, services, features, and solutions.

- Embrace technology advancements, digital transformation, and IoT (Internet of Things) to enhance offerings and customer experiences.

4. **Brand Identity and Positioning**

   - Evolve brand identity, values, messaging, and positioning to reflect evolving market trends, customer values, and competitive landscape.

   - Rebranding, brand refresh, or brand extensions can reinvigorate brand perception and attract new audiences.

5. **Collaboration and Partnerships**

   - Collaborate with industry partners, startups, innovators, and experts to access new ideas, technologies, resources, and market opportunities.

   - Joint ventures, co-creation projects, and innovation hubs foster creativity, knowledge sharing, and cross-functional collaboration.

6. **Agility and Experimentation**

   - Foster a culture of agility, experimentation, and risk-taking within the organization to encourage innovation and continuous improvement.

- Implement agile methodologies, rapid prototyping, and iterative development to test and iterate new ideas and concepts quickly.

7. **Marketing and Communication**

   - Develop innovative marketing campaigns, storytelling, and content strategies that resonate with target audiences and showcase brand evolution.

   - Leverage digital marketing, social media, influencer partnerships, and experiential marketing to amplify brand innovation and reach.

 Benefits of Brand Evolution and Innovation

1. **Competitive Differentiation:** Innovative brands differentiate themselves from competitors, creating a unique selling proposition and competitive advantage.

2. **Customer Loyalty and Advocacy:** Brand evolution and innovation build customer loyalty, satisfaction, and advocacy through novel experiences, products, and solutions.

3. **Market Expansion: New** offerings and innovations open doors to new markets, customer segments, revenue streams, and business opportunities.

4. **Brand Resilience:** Adaptive brands are resilient to market changes, disruptions, and challenges, ensuring sustainability and long-term success.

5. **Organizational Growth: A** culture of innovation and brand evolution fosters employee engagement, creativity, and organizational growth.

By embracing brand evolution and innovation as strategic imperatives, brands can stay ahead of the curve, delight customers, drive growth, and achieve sustainable success in rapidly evolving markets.

CONCLUSION

In conclusion, "Brand Brilliance: Building a Lasting Identity in the Marketplace" illuminates the transformative power of strategic brand management and innovation. Throughout this journey, we have explored the intricacies of crafting a compelling brand identity, navigating competitive landscapes, leveraging customer experiences, and sustaining relevance over time.

The essence of brand brilliance lies not only in creating captivating logos or captivating marketing campaigns but in fostering deep connections with customers, embodying authenticity, and delivering exceptional value consistently. By embracing innovation, adaptation, and customer-centricity, brands can carve their unique space in the marketplace, resonate with audiences, and foster enduring relationships built on trust and loyalty.

As we navigate the ever-evolving landscape of business and consumer dynamics, remember that a brand's journey is not static but dynamic—a continuous evolution guided by strategic insights, market intelligence, and a relentless pursuit of excellence. May the principles, strategies, and insights shared in this book inspire you to unlock the full potential of your brand, create lasting impact, and illuminate the path to brand brilliance in the marketplace.

Here's to building brands that shine bright, resonate deeply, and stand the test of time. Thank you for embarking on this enlightening journey of brand brilliance with us.

www.ingramcontent.com/pod-product-compliance
Lightning Source LLC
Chambersburg PA
CBHW070205230526
45471CB00002B/822